PHILOSOPHICAL QUESTIONS FOR CURIOUS MINDS

497 PHILOSOPHICAL QUESTIONS ABOUT PERSONAL IDENTITY, HUMAN NATURE, LANGUAGE AND COMMUNICATION, GENDER AND SEXUALITY, ARTIFICIAL INTELLIGENCE, AND MORE

PHILOSOPHY FOR THE CURIOUS
BOOK 2

LUKE MARSH

BOOK BOUND STUDIOS

Copyright © 2023 by Luke Marsh

All rights reserved. No part of this book may be reproduced, stored in a retrieval system, or transmitted in any form or by any means, electronic, mechanical, photocopying, recording, or otherwise, without the prior written permission of the publisher, Book Bound Studios.

The information contained in this book is based on the author's personal experiences and research. While every effort has been made to ensure the accuracy of the information presented, the author and publisher cannot be held responsible for any errors or omissions.

This book is intended for general informational purposes only and is not a substitute for professional medical, legal, or financial advice. If you have specific questions about any medical, legal, or financial matters matters, you should consult with a qualified healthcare professional, attorney, or financial advisor.

Book Bound Studios is not affiliated with any product or vendor mentioned in this book. The views expressed in this book are those of the author and do not necessarily reflect the views of Book Bound Studios.

"The unexamined life is not worth living."

— SOCRATES

CONTENTS

Introduction   vii

1. Personal Identity   1
2. Human Nature   11
3. Language and Communication   21
4. Gender and Sexuality   31
5. Race and Ethnicity   41
6. Social and Economic Justice   51
7. Environmental Ethics   61
8. Artificial Intelligence   73
9. Time and Space   83
10. The Meaning of Life   93

Afterword   103
About the Author   105
From the Author   107

INTRODUCTION

Welcome to *Philosophical Questions for Curious Minds*! This book is the second in its series, *"Philosophy for the Curious"*—a collection of thought-provoking questions designed to stimulate the mind and encourage critical thinking and self-reflection. It covers a wide range of philosophical topics, including personal identity, human nature, language and communication, gender and sexuality, and the meaning of life. Each topic includes an introduction, philosophical questions, random facts and a popular paradox. So whether you're an experienced philosopher or someone who loves to ponder deep questions, this book has something for you. So grab a pen and paper, and get ready to dive into some of the most interesting and challenging questions humanity has ever asked.

1
PERSONAL IDENTITY

Personal identity is a concept that is central to our sense of self and our place in the world. It involves the question of what makes us the same person over time and what factors contribute to our identities. This complex and multifaceted concept has been the subject of much contemplation and debate among philosophers. In this chapter, we will explore 50 philosophical questions about personal identity. These questions range from the abstract to the concrete. They touch upon various topics, including the nature of the self, memory, continuity, and the relationship between personal identity and the body. Whether you are a seasoned philosopher or curious about the world around you, we hope these questions will stimulate your thinking and help you better understand the complex and multifaceted concept of personal identity.

Philosophical Questions About Personal Identity

I'll start us off by answering the first three questions. The rest are all up to you to solve. I have no doubt that you'll do a great job. Time to shine!

What makes a human unique?

From a biological perspective, humans are unique due to their highly developed brains and ability to use complex language. Humans are the only species to have developed complex cultures, societies, and technologies.

From a psychological perspective, humans are unique due to their ability to experience a wide range of emotions and their capacity for self-reflection and introspection. Humans can also make choices based on their values and beliefs, which sets them apart from other animals.

Is it possible to exist without a sense of self?

On the one hand, it is possible to exist without a sense of self. Many philosophers and spiritual traditions have argued that the sense of self is an illusion and that true enlightenment or liberation involves letting go of the ego and the illusion of self. In some forms of meditation and spiritual practice, practitioners aim to experience a state of "no self," in which they let go of their attachment to their thoughts, emotions, and sense of self.

On the other hand, it is not possible to exist without a sense of self. The sense of self is an integral part of the human experience. It is difficult to imagine what it would be like to completely let go of the ego. Our sense of self is closely tied to our personal identity, and it plays a central role in our ability to make decisions, form relationships, and interact with the world around us. Without a sense of self, we would lose our sense of agency and ability to navigate the world.

Is our identity defined by our memories?

On the one hand, our identity is largely defined by our memories. Our memories make up a significant part of who we are, shaping how we perceive ourselves and the world around us. Our memories influence our beliefs, values, and behaviors and help form our sense of self. Without our memories, we would not be able to understand our past experiences or make sense of the present.

On the other hand, our identity is not solely defined by our memories. While memories are an important part of our identity, they are not the only factor that shapes who we are. Our identity is also shaped by our genetics, environment, and choices. We may have memories that conflict with our current beliefs or values, and it is up to us to decide which memories are most important to us in shaping our identity. Additionally, our identity is flexible and can change over time as we have new experiences and make new choices.

Don't let setbacks and challenges get you down. Just remember that every obstacle is an opportunity to show off your problem-solving skills and become a stronger, more resilient person. And if all else fails, just remember that wine and cheese make everything better. Keep going!

. . .

Is personal identity inextricably linked to physicality?

What is the relationship between our physical and psychological identities?

Is it possible to change one's identity?

What is the definition of a "true" self?

Does our identity shape our behavior, or is it predetermined?

Is identity a result of our experiences or an innate quality?

Is identity something that is created or discovered?

Is our identity determined by our environment or by our choices?

Is our identity the same across different contexts?

How does our personal identity affect our interactions with others?

Is personal identity a result of nature or nurture?

. . .

How does our culture shape our identity?

How does one's identity evolve over time?

Does our identity carry over from one life to the next?

Are we more than the sum of our parts?

Is personal identity an illusion?

How do our choices reflect our identity?

Does our identity change with our beliefs?

Is personal identity affected by our values?

How does one's identity change when confronted with a new environment?

Is identity something that can be lost?

Is identity a social construction?

10 Random Facts About Personal Identity

1. The concept of personal identity has been a topic of philosophical debate for centuries, with different philosophers offering different definitions and theories.
2. One influential theory of personal identity is known as the "physical criterion," which states that a person's identity is determined by their physical body.
3. Another theory is the "psychological criterion," which suggests that a person's identity is based on their thoughts, memories, and personality.
4. Some philosophers have argued that personal identity is a combination of both physical and psychological factors.
5. Our sense of personal identity is closely tied to our sense of self, which is our subjective experience of being unique.
6. Our sense of self can be influenced by various factors, including our culture, upbringing, and personal experiences.
7. Some people may have a strong sense of personal identity. In contrast, others may feel that their identity is more fluid and changeable.
8. Some people may feel that their personal identity is closely tied to their profession or societal role. In contrast, others may feel that their identity is more personal and individual.
9. Our personal identity can change over time as we gain new experiences and insights and our priorities and values evolve.
10. Our personal identity is often reflected in how we present ourselves to the world through our appearance, behavior, and choices.

More Philosophical Questions About Personal Identity

Is personal identity a matter of perception or reality?

. . .

Philosophical Questions for Curious Minds

Does our identity depend on the opinions of others?

Is our identity shaped by our relationships?

What is the purpose of personal identity?

Is personal identity determined by our physical appearance?

How does one's identity shape their future?

Does our identity remain the same over time?

Is personal identity predetermined or malleable?

Is personal identity a reflection of our behavior?

Is identity a matter of choice or chance?

How does our identity affect our understanding of the world?

Is identity something that can be changed?

Is personal identity a form of power?

Does one's identity remain the same across different cultures?

Is identity something that is inherited or learned?

Does our identity define our purpose in life?

Is identity an individual experience or a shared experience?

Is personal identity a universal concept?

How does our identity influence our decision-making?

Does our identity shape our morality?

Does our identity depend on our environment?

How does the media affect our identity?

Does our identity define our relationships?

Is identity a form of expression?

How does our identity shape our view of the world?

A Paradox About Personal Identity

One famous paradox about personal identity is the *"Ship of Theseus"* paradox. This paradox raises the question of whether a ship, which has had all of its component parts replaced over time, is still the same as the original.

In other words, if every piece of wood, nail, and rope on the ship has been replaced, is the ship that remains the same ship as it was originally? If it is not the same ship, when did it cease to be the same ship? If it is still the same ship, what makes it the same if all of its physical parts are different?

This paradox can be applied to personal identity as well. If every cell in a person's body is replaced over time, is that person still the same person as they were original? If not, then when did they cease to be the same person? If they are still the same person, what makes them the same person if all of their physical parts are different?

This paradox raises questions about the nature of personal identity and what, if anything, makes a person the same individual over time. Furthermore, it suggests that our physical bodies may not be the most important factor in determining our personal identity and that other, more abstract aspects of ourselves persist over time and contribute to our sense of self.

2
HUMAN NATURE

Human nature is a concept that has been the subject of much contemplation and debate among philosophers, theologians, and scientists. It involves the question of what characteristics and traits are uniquely human and how they shape our behavior and place in the world. Moreover, this complex and multifaceted concept has implications for our understanding of the self, society, and the human condition. In this chapter, we will explore 50 philosophical questions about human nature. These questions range from the abstract to the concrete. They touch upon various topics, including the nature of the self, consciousness, morality, and the relationship between humans and other animals. Whether you are a seasoned philosopher or curious about the world around you, we hope these questions will stimulate your thinking and help you better understand the complex and multifaceted concept of human nature.

Philosophical Questions About Human Nature

I'll take on the first three questions to get the ball rolling. The rest are all yours to handle. I have full faith in your problem-solving abilities. Go ahead and show me what you can do!

What is the purpose of human existence?

From a religious perspective, the purpose of human existence may be seen as fulfilling a certain role or mission given by a higher power, such as serving God or living according to a certain spiritual doctrine.

From a secular perspective, the purpose of human existence may be more centered on individual fulfillment and the pursuit of personal goals and happiness. This could include pursuing one's passions, forming meaningful relationships, and contributing to the greater good.

What is the nature of the human soul?

The human soul is a metaphysical concept that is eternal and immortal. It is the essence of a person's being and gives us consciousness and free will. Some believe the soul is the seat of our emotions, thoughts, and personality and separates us from other animals.

The human soul is a purely material entity with no inherent spiritual or metaphysical properties. It is simply the result of complex neural processes within the brain. According to this perspective, the concept of a soul is a cultural and philosophical construct, and there is no scientific evidence to support its existence.

Is there innate goodness in human nature?

On the one hand, there is an innate goodness in human nature. Proponents of this perspective might argue that humans are naturally empathetic, cooperative, and compassionate and that these traits are evident from a young age. They might point to research on prosocial behaviors in infants and young children, such as the tendency to help others and share resources, as evidence of an inherent moral sense. They also argue that cultural and societal influences can either enhance or detract from this innate goodness but that it is a fundamental part of being human.

On the other hand, there is no innate goodness in human nature. Those who hold this perspective might argue that humans are not naturally good but driven by selfish desires and a need to protect their interests. They might point to examples of violence, aggression, and other harmful behaviors as evidence that humans are not inherently moral. They also argue that innate goodness is a cultural or societal construct and that individuals learn to be good through socialization and conditioning.

Don't give up, even when things get tough. Just keep reminding yourself that you're one step closer to achieving your goals. And if all else fails, just take a break and watch some cat videos on YouTube. They always seem to put a smile on my face. Keep going!

. . .

Is human nature determined by biology or environment?

What is the nature of human morality?

Is human nature fundamentally selfish or selfless?

Is human life essentially good or evil?

Is human nature essentially rational or irrational?

Is it possible to have a universal morality?

Is human nature inherently creative or destructive?

Is the human capacity for empathy essential to human nature?

Is human nature cooperative or competitive?

What is the relationship between human nature and technology?

Is human freedom an illusion or a reality?

Is human nature determined by biology or culture?

. . .

Is human nature essentially selfish or altruistic?

Is human nature determined by nature or nurture?

What is the role of free will in human nature?

Is human nature essentially good or evil?

Is human nature determined by biological instinct or conscious choices?

Do our motivations and desires determine our human nature?

Is human nature shaped more by our individual experiences or collective experience?

Is human nature determined by our social environment or individual experiences?

Is it possible to make moral decisions without referencing a predetermined code of ethics?

Is human nature determined by instinct or by reason?

Is human nature determined by our conscious or unconscious minds?

10 Random Facts About Human Nature

1. Humans are the only primates with a prominent chin, resulting from our ancestors eating a more varied diet that included harder foods.
2. The average person walks three times around the world in a lifetime.
3. The human nose can detect over 1 trillion different scents.
4. The human brain is the most complex organ in the body and contains more neurons than stars in the Milky Way.
5. The average person spends about a third of their life asleep.
6. Humans are the only animals that can produce emotional tears.
7. The human eye can distinguish between over 10 million different colors.
8. The human heart pumps enough blood daily to fill a tanker truck.
9. The average person has over 100,000 hairs on their head.
10. Humans are the only animals that can produce a genuine smile and not just a sign of aggression or submission.

More Philosophical Questions About Human Nature

What is the role of emotions in understanding human nature?

Is human nature determined by our genetic makeup or by our environment?

Is human nature predetermined or malleable?

. . .

Is human nature determined by our individual experiences or collective experience?

Is human nature determined by our culture or biology?

Is the human capacity for compassion essential to our nature?

Is human nature determined by the collective or the individual?

Is the human capacity for love essential to our nature?

Is human nature determined by our choices or by our circumstances?

Is human nature determined by our environment or by our biology?

Is human nature determined by our natural or external environment?

Is human nature naturally peaceful or naturally violent?

Is human nature determined by our genetic makeup or culture?

Is the human capacity for empathy essential to our nature?

Is the human capacity for creativity essential to our nature?

. . .

Is the human capacity for language essential to our nature?

Is the human capacity for reason essential to our nature?

Is the human capacity for judgment essential to our nature?

Is the human capacity for morality essential to our nature?

Is the human capacity for free will essential to our nature?

Is the human capacity for intelligence essential to our nature?

Is the human capacity for love essential to our nature?

Is the human capacity for cooperation essential to our nature?

Is the human capacity for self-awareness essential to our nature?

A Paradox About Human Nature

One paradox of human nature is that while we crave connection and belonging with others and are social creatures who rely on each other for emotional and practical support, we also value our individuality and independence and desire to express ourselves and pursue our own interests without interference. This tension between the need for connection and the desire for independence can create conflicts and misunderstandings within relationships and society as we try to balance these conflicting desires. Yet, despite this paradox, humans can navigate these conflicting desires and find ways to form meaningful relationships and connections while maintaining their individuality.

3
LANGUAGE AND COMMUNICATION

Language and communication are fundamental to the human experience. They allow us to express our thoughts, feelings, and ideas and connect with others meaningfully. But language and communication are also complex and multifaceted phenomena that have puzzled philosophers for centuries. What is the nature of language, and how does it function? How do we communicate meaning, and what are the limits of language? This chapter will explore 50 philosophical questions about language and communication. These questions range from the abstract to the concrete. They touch upon various topics, including the nature of meaning, the relationship between language and thought, and the role of language in shaping our understanding of the world. Whether you are a linguist or curious about the world around you, we hope these questions will stimulate your thinking and help you better understand the complex and multifaceted phenomena of language and communication.

Philosophical Questions About Language and Communication

I'll answer the first three questions to get the conversation going. The rest are all up to you. I'm sure you'll do a fantastic job. Time to put your skills to the test!

Is language a tool for communication or a barrier to understanding?

On the one hand, a language is a tool for communication. Language is a system of symbols and rules that allows people to communicate with one another. It is a tool that enables people to express their thoughts, ideas, and feelings to others and to understand the thoughts, ideas, and feelings of others. With language, it would be easier for people to share information and ideas and build relationships.

On the other hand, language is a barrier to understanding. While language can be a tool for communication, it can also be a barrier to understanding. This is because different people speak different languages, and only some are fluent in the same language. This can create communication barriers, leading to misunderstandings and difficulty comprehending each other's thoughts and ideas. Additionally, even within the same language, different dialects and ways of speaking can make it difficult for people to fully understand one another.

What is the role of language in forming and maintaining relationships?

Language plays a crucial role in forming and maintaining relationships because it allows people to communicate and express their thoughts, feelings, and needs to one another. It is the primary means by which people establish and maintain social bonds, build trust, and negotiate the terms of their relationships. Without language, it would be extremely difficult, if not impossible, for people to form and maintain relationships with one another.

Some might argue that language is less important than other factors in forming and maintaining relationships. They point to nonverbal communication, such as body language, gestures, and facial expressions, as being more influential in this regard. They might also argue that shared interests, values, and experiences are more important in forming and maintaining relationships than language. While language is an important factor in relationships, it may not be the most decisive one for everyone.

How does language influence our perception of reality?

On the one hand, language greatly influences our perception of reality because it shapes how we think and understand the world around us. The words we use to describe our experiences and the concepts we have for understanding those experiences shape how we perceive and make sense of things. For example, we only have words for a limited range of colors. In that case, we may not be able to perceive or describe certain shades outside of that range. Similarly, suppose a language needs words for certain concepts. In that case, it is easier for speakers of that language to think about or comprehend those concepts.

On the other hand, language does not completely determine our perception of reality but reflects and reflects upon it. In other words, our perception of reality exists independently of language, and a language is simply a tool we use to express and communicate our perceptions. Language can indeed influence our thoughts and understanding. Still, it is not the sole determinant of what we perceive or how we perceive it. Our senses and experiences also play a role in shaping our perception of reality.

You may not be where you want to be right now, but that's okay. Every journey has its ups and downs. Just keep moving forward and trust that you'll get to where you're meant to be. And if all else fails, remember that napping is a completely valid way to recharge your batteries. Keep going!

What is the difference between language and communication?

Does language define our identity?

Is language a reflection of our culture and society?

How does our language reflect our values and beliefs?

How does language influence our understanding of the world?

Is language a human construct or an innate ability?

Does language limit our communication capabilities?

Philosophical Questions for Curious Minds

. . .

Is language more important than the content of the communication?

Is language necessary for communication?

What is the power of language in creating and conveying meaning?

How does language shape our views of the world?

Does language have the power to shape our thoughts and emotions?

How does language shape our understanding of truth?

Is communication a form of expressing language, or is language a form of expressing communication?

How can we use language to better communicate our thoughts and feelings?

Is language a tool of oppression or liberation?

How does language shape our identity and sense of belonging?

How does language shape our understanding of gender roles?

. . .

What is the relationship between language, culture, and power?

Is language a reflection of our mental processes?

How does language influence our behavior and interactions?

10 Random Facts About Language and Communication

1. There are more than 7,000 languages spoken in the world today.
2. The oldest written language is Sumerian, dating back to around 3500 BCE.
3. The most widely spoken language in the world is Mandarin Chinese, which is spoken by around 1.4 billion people.
4. English has the largest vocabulary of any language, with around 170,000 words.
5. The longest word in the English language is pneumonoultramicroscopicsilicovolcanoconiosis, which refers to a lung disease caused by inhaling very fine particles of silica.
6. The shortest complete sentence in the English language is "I am," which contains only two letters.
7. Many languages do not use written words, including some Indigenous languages in Australia and the Americas, which rely on body language and facial expressions to convey meaning.
8. American Sign Language (ASL) is a complete, natural language used by people who are deaf or hard of hearing. It has its own grammar, vocabulary, and syntax and is not simply a representation of spoken English.

9. Some languages, such as Hopi and Pirahã, do not have words for numbers and do not use a counting system.
10. The study of language and communication is known as linguistics, an interdisciplinary field that includes elements of psychology, sociology, anthropology, and computer science.

More Philosophical Questions About Language and Communication

What is the relationship between language and truth?

How does language shape our understanding of morality?

Is language an expression of our individuality or collective identity?

How does language shape our understanding of the world?

Does language have the power to create social change?

What is the relationship between language and memory?

Are words the only way to communicate?

How does language shape our understanding of history?

Does the use of language limit our ability to think critically?

. . .

Is language an art or a science?

How does language shape our understanding of reality?

What is the relationship between language and thought?

How does language affect our ability to think abstractly?

Is language an expression of our emotions?

What is the relationship between language and identity?

Is language an expression of our beliefs?

What is the relationship between language and culture?

How does language shape our understanding of the world?

How does language influence our ability to make decisions?

What is the relationship between language and power?

Is language a reflection of our values and beliefs?

. . .

Does language have the power to shape our behavior?

Is language a tool of oppression or of liberation?

How does language shape our understanding of truth?

How does language impact our understanding of the past?

Is language an expression of our collective identity?

A Paradox About Language and Communication

"The Paradox of Communication" is a paradox that arises when we try to communicate something to someone else. The paradox is that to communicate something, we must use language. Still, language is something that we are trying to communicate.

For example, suppose I want to communicate the concept of "red" to you. In that case, I might say, "the color red is a bright, warm color that is often associated with passion and emotion." However, to understand this statement, you must already have a basic understanding of language and its rules, as well as a shared understanding of the meaning of the words "color," "red," "bright," "warm," and so on.

This paradox can be seen as a vicious circle, as we are constantly using language to communicate something while at the same time relying on language to understand what is being communicated. It highlights the importance of shared understanding, language, and communication in building and maintaining relationships.

4
GENDER AND SEXUALITY

Gender and sexuality are complex and multifaceted concepts that have been the subject of much contemplation and debate among philosophers, theologians, and social scientists. They involve how we understand and experience our own and others' genders and sexualities and how these experiences are shaped by cultural, social, and political forces. This chapter will explore 50 philosophical questions about gender and sexuality. These questions range from the abstract to the concrete. They touch upon various topics, including the nature of gender and sexuality, the relationship between gender and identity, and the role of culture and power in shaping our understanding of gender and sexuality. Whether you are a scholar in this field or simply someone curious about the world around you, we hope these questions will stimulate your thinking and help you better understand the complex and multifaceted concepts of gender and sexuality.

Philosophical Questions About Gender and Sexuality

I'll start us off by answering the first three questions. The rest are all up to you. I have full confidence in your abilities to handle the rest on your own.

What is the relationship between gender and sexuality?

From a biological perspective, gender and sexuality are often seen as separate concepts. Gender refers to the physical and physiological characteristics that define men and women. At the same time, sexuality encompasses a person's sexual identity, attractions, and behaviors. These concepts can intersect and influence each other, but they are not the same.

From a social and cultural perspective, gender and sexuality are often closely intertwined. In many societies, certain gender roles and expectations are imposed on people based on their biological sex. These roles and expectations can shape a person's sexual identity and behaviors. For example, in some cultures, men are expected to be sexually aggressive and dominant. In contrast, women are expected to be sexually passive and submissive. These societal norms can significantly impact an individual's sense of self and relationships with others.

Is gender a social construct?

On the one hand, gender is a social construct. It is a set of societal expectations and norms assigned to people based on their perceived sex. These expectations and norms vary across different cultures and have changed over time, which suggests that they are not inherent or biological but rather constructed by society.

On the other hand, gender is not a social construct. There are inherent biological differences between men and women, such as hormones and reproductive anatomy, that cannot be ignored or denied. While cultural expectations and norms may vary, these fundamental biological differences exist and shape an individual's experience and expression of gender.

What is the purpose of gender roles?

One perspective on the purpose of gender roles is that they serve as a social and cultural construct, defining and distinguishing the roles, behaviors, and expectations of men and women in a given society. These roles can vary significantly across different cultures and periods and may be based on various factors, including biology, economics, politics, and religion. Gender roles often shape an individual's identity, relationships, and opportunities. As a result, they can have a powerful influence on socialization and development. Some people argue that gender roles help to create a sense of order and predictability in society and provide a foundation for social norms and expectations.

Another perspective on the purpose of gender roles is that they are a form of social control and oppression used to maintain and reinforce power dynamics between men and women. This view suggests that gender roles are not natural or inevitable but are created and enforced by society to maintain certain groups' dominance and limit others' opportunities and freedoms. In addition, some people argue that gender roles are used to justify discrimination and violence against women and gender non-conforming individuals and that they limit the ability of individuals to fully express themselves and pursue their own goals and interests. From this perspective, the purpose of gender roles is to maintain the status quo and to prevent social change.

When the going gets tough, just remember that you're tougher. You've got this! Now go out there and give it your all. And if all else fails, just remember that you can always order a pizza and start again tomorrow. Keep going!

How does gender affect the way we view ourselves?

Is gender identity inherent or something acquired?

What is the role of gender in shaping societal values?

Are gender roles necessary for a functioning society?

How is gender related to power dynamics?

What is the role of gender in determining our personalities?

How do gender norms influence how we interact?

. . .

Is gender an innate or learned trait?

How does gender influence our expectations of each other?

Is gender a binary construct, or is there more to it?

How has the concept of gender evolved over time?

How do gender roles impact our relationships?

Are gender roles a reflection of societal values?

How can we challenge existing gender roles?

How does gender intersect with race and ethnicity?

How does gender play a role in our understanding of sexuality?

What is the role of gender in creating our identity?

How does gender shape our sense of self?

How does gender affect our decision-making?

. . .

Are gender roles determined by biology or culture?

How does gender impact our mental health?

Are there any universal gender roles?

10 Random Facts About Gender and Sexuality

1. People use more than 50 different terms to describe their gender identity.
2. Gender is different from biological sex, which refers to the physical characteristics that make someone male, female, or intersex.
3. The term "transgender" refers to people who identify with a gender different from the one they were assigned at birth.
4. Sexual orientation refers to a person's emotional, romantic, and sexual attraction to other people.
5. The term "queer" is used by some people to describe their sexual orientation or gender identity, as it can be more inclusive than other terms.
6. A person's sexual orientation or gender identity can change throughout their lifetime.
7. Many cultures have traditionally recognized a third gender, including the hijra in India and Bangladesh, the muxes in Mexico, and the two-spirit people in many Indigenous North American cultures.
8. There is no link between a person's sexual orientation or gender identity and their ability to perform a job or task.
9. The World Health Organization removed "homosexuality" from its list of mental disorders in 1990.
10. "LGBT" is an acronym for lesbian, gay, bisexual, and transgender. Many other acronyms have been created to be

more inclusive, such as LGBTQ+ (which stands for lesbian, gay, bisexual, transgender, and queer) and LGBTQIA+ (which stands for lesbian, gay, bisexual, transgender, queer, intersex, and asexual).

More Philosophical Questions About Gender and Sexuality

How does gender shape our opinions and beliefs?

How do gender roles affect our personal development?

How does gender influence our self-esteem?

How does society view gender and sexuality?

How can we create a more equitable society where gender is not a factor?

How does gender shape our view of the world?

How has the understanding of gender and sexuality changed over time?

How do gender and sexuality intersect with other aspects of identity?

What is the impact of gender on our physical and mental health?

How does gender inform our relationships with others?

. . .

How does gender identity affect our self-expression?

What is the role of gender in forming our identities?

How do gender norms influence our behavior?

How can we create a society where gender is respected and accepted?

Why is gender still seen as a binary construct?

Is gender a biological or social construct?

How does gender impact the way we interact with each other?

What is the role of gender in creating our values and beliefs?

How can we create a more gender-inclusive society?

How has technology changed the way we view gender and sexuality?

How does gender influence our relationships?

. . .

How does gender impact our economic choices?

What is the role of education in reshaping gender norms?

How does gender affect our communication styles?

How does gender shape our understanding of the world?

A Paradox About Gender and Sexuality

One popular paradox about gender and sexuality is the idea of the *"gender binary."* The gender binary is the belief that there are only two genders, male and female, and that everyone must be either one or the other. However, this belief is paradoxical because it ignores the existence of nonbinary and gender-nonconforming individuals who do not identify as exclusively male or female. This paradox is often referred to as the "gender binary paradox."

The gender binary paradox is problematic because it reinforces harmful societal norms and stereotypes about gender and sexuality, and it can lead to discrimination and marginalization of those who do not conform to these norms. It is important to recognize that gender and sexuality are complex and fluid concepts and that there are many ways in which people can identify and express their gender and sexuality. By acknowledging and embracing the diversity of gender and sexual identities, we can work towards a more inclusive and accepting society.

5
RACE AND ETHNICITY

Race and ethnicity are complex and multifaceted concepts that have been the subject of much contemplation and debate among philosophers, theologians, and social scientists. They involve how we understand and experience our and others' racial and ethnic identities and how they are shaped by cultural, social, and political forces. This chapter will explore 50 philosophical questions about race and ethnicity. These questions range from the abstract to the concrete. They touch upon various topics, including the nature of race and ethnicity, the relationship between race and identity, and the role of culture and power in shaping our understanding of race and ethnicity. Whether you are a scholar in this field or someone curious about the world around you, we hope these questions will stimulate your thinking and help you better understand the complex and multifaceted concepts of race and ethnicity.

Philosophical Questions About Race and Ethnicity

I'll start us off by answering the first three questions. The rest are all up to you to solve. Don't let the challenge intimidate you. You have the skills and knowledge to succeed. Go out there and give it your best shot. I have full faith in you!

Do race and ethnicity directly affect an individual's sense of identity?

On the one hand, race and ethnicity can directly affect an individual's sense of identity. These factors are often closely tied to an individual's cultural background and can shape their beliefs, values, and experiences. For example, someone raised in a predominantly African American community may have a different sense of identity than someone raised in a predominantly white community due to the different cultural norms and experiences that they are exposed to. Similarly, someone of Hispanic heritage may have a strong sense of cultural identity influenced by their ethnicity.

On the other hand, race and ethnicity do not directly affect an individual's sense of identity. While these factors may play a role in shaping an individual's cultural background and experiences, many other factors can also contribute to an individual's sense of identity. For example, an individual's family, education, personal interests, and values can all contribute to their sense of identity. Additionally, an individual's identity can change and evolve regardless of race or ethnicity.

Is the concept of race a social construct or a biological reality?

On the one hand, the concept of race is a social construct.

This perspective argues that the concept of race is a human invention and does not have any biological basis. The idea of race was created by societies to categorize and distinguish people based on physical characteristics such as skin color, eye shape, and facial features. However, these physical characteristics do not accurately reflect the complex genetic makeup of an individual. Moreover, they do not correspond to any inherent biological differences. As such, race is a social construct used to group people together based on arbitrary and subjective criteria.

On the other hand, the concept of race is a biological reality.

This perspective argues that race is a biologically based phenomenon reflecting genetic differences between different populations. It is believed that these differences arose due to the process of evolution, which resulted in the development of distinct physical characteristics in different populations that adapted to their specific environments. This perspective argues that these physical differences indicate genetic differences between different races. That race is, therefore, a biological reality.

Are individuals responsible for the racial biases they hold?

On the one hand, individuals are responsible for their racial biases because they can choose their thoughts and beliefs. No one is born with inherent biases, and it is up to each individual to actively work to recognize and challenge any prejudices they may have.

On the other hand, individuals are not solely responsible for their racial biases because biases and prejudices are often learned and perpetuated through societal messages and cultural conditioning. While individuals have the power to challenge and work to unlearn these biases, they are not solely responsible for their existence. Therefore, it is important to recognize the larger societal and systemic factors contributing to the perpetuation of biases and work toward addressing them.

Don't let setbacks and challenges hold you back. They're just temporary obstacles on the road to success. And if you ever feel like giving up, just remember that there's a tub of ice cream waiting for you at the finish line. Keep going!

Does the concept of race limit our ability to see people as individuals?

Is it possible to be colorblind in a racially divided society?

Is race meaningful in understanding a person's unique experience?

Is it possible to transcend race and ethnicity?

Are traditional ideas of race and ethnicity outdated?

How does power shape how we think about race and ethnicity?

Is it possible to think about race and ethnicity in a non-binary way?

To what extent do our racial identities determine our life outcomes?

How does race intersect with gender, class, and other social identities?

Does race have the power to unite or divide us?

What is the impact of racial discrimination on individuals and communities?

How are race and ethnicity represented in the media?

How do people of color experience racism differently than white people?

How do we define race and ethnicity in the 21st century?

Are there any benefits to identifying with a particular race or ethnicity?

How does racism manifest in our everyday lives?

How can we use race and ethnicity to better understand our world?

What is the difference between race and ethnicity, and why is it important?

What is the role of privilege in the context of race and ethnicity?

LUKE MARSH

. . .

How do we address issues of racial injustice in our society?

How does the history of slavery and colonialism shape our understanding of race today?

How do we recognize and challenge our racial biases?

10 Random Facts About Race and Ethnicity

1. Race and ethnicity are social constructs that categorize people based on physical characteristics, such as skin color, hair texture, and facial features.
2. Race and ethnicity are not based on scientific or biological criteria, and there is significant genetic diversity within each racial and ethnic group.
3. The concept of race has a long and complex history. It has been used to justify discrimination and oppression in many societies.
4. Ethnicity refers to cultural characteristics, such as language, traditions, and shared history passed down within a group.
5. There is no consensus on how many races or ethnicities exist, and the categories used to define them vary from one society to another.
6. Some people may identify with more than one race or ethnicity, and some may not identify with any particular group.
7. In many societies, race and ethnicity intersect with other forms of social inequality, such as class, gender, and sexuality.

8. The relationship between race and ethnicity can be complex, and people may experience discrimination or privilege based on both factors.
9. Many people are active in social justice movements that seek to challenge and dismantle systems of racial and ethnic inequality.
10. Race and ethnicity are important aspects of personal identity and can influence an individual's experiences and perspectives.

More Philosophical Questions About Race and Ethnicity

Is there such a thing as a "post-racial" society?

What is the relationship between race and racism?

Does the concept of race still have a place in our modern, multicultural society?

What are the effects of racial stereotyping, and how can we combat them?

Are there any social benefits to maintaining a racial identity?

What is education's role in addressing race and ethnicity?

How can we create an inclusive environment for all racial and ethnic backgrounds?

. . .

How do our views on race and ethnicity evolve over time?

Is it possible to have a meaningful dialogue about race without offending others?

How can we move past racial divisions to create a more equitable society?

How do our perceptions of race and ethnicity change as we gain new perspectives?

How does the concept of race affect our understanding of history?

How can we use race and ethnicity to bridge cultural divides?

How does our understanding of race and ethnicity shape our cultural values?

Is it possible to separate race and ethnicity from culture?

What is the impact of globalization on race and ethnicity?

How can race and ethnicity be used as empowerment tools?

Are there any universal experiences related to race and ethnicity?

. . .

Are there any social or economic implications of racial identity?

Is racial identity something that can be chosen, or is it predetermined?

Does the concept of race create a divide between different groups of people?

How do we balance the need for diversity with the need for inclusion?

Is there a difference between race and ethnicity in terms of their effects on our lives?

How can we use race and ethnicity to foster understanding and acceptance?

What role do race and ethnicity play in understanding social and political power?

A Paradox About Race and Ethnicity

One popular paradox about race and ethnicity is the "diversity paradox." This paradox refers to the idea that diversity is often seen as a positive thing and is actively sought after in many settings (such as schools and workplaces). However, it can also lead to increased conflict and tension.

For example, in a diverse group of employees, there may be a greater potential for misunderstandings and miscommunications due to differences in cultural backgrounds and experiences. Additionally, research has shown that people often have a natural preference for others similar to themselves, which can lead to the formation of homogenous groups within a diverse setting.

This can create a dynamic where, despite diversity, there still needs to be true integration and understanding between different groups. In other words, the existence of diversity does not automatically lead to harmony and understanding.

This paradox highlights the complexity of issues related to race and ethnicity. It suggests that simply promoting diversity is not enough to address the underlying issues that lead to inequality and conflict. Instead, actively creating a more inclusive and understanding society is important.

6
SOCIAL AND ECONOMIC JUSTICE

Social and economic justice are complex and multifaceted concepts that have been the subject of much contemplation and debate among philosophers, theologians, and social scientists. They involve how we should distribute resources and power within society and what kind of society would be most fair and just for all its members. This chapter will explore 50 philosophical questions about social and economic justice. These questions range from the abstract to the concrete, and they touch upon a variety of topics, including equality, freedom, democracy, and the role of the state in promoting justice. Whether you are a scholar in this field or curious about the world around you, we hope these questions will stimulate your thinking and help you better understand the complex and multifaceted concepts of social and economic justice.

Philosophical Questions About Social and Economic Justice

I'll take on the first three questions to get the ball rolling. The rest are all up to you. Don't be afraid to take on the challenge. You have the capability to succeed. Go out there and give it your all. I believe in you!

What is the definition of social and economic justice?

On the one hand, social and economic justice refers to the fair and just distribution of resources, opportunities, and privileges within a society. It involves ensuring that all individuals, regardless of their background or circumstances, have equal access to the same opportunities and can fully participate in the social and economic systems that shape their lives. This includes access to education, healthcare, housing, employment, fair wages, benefits, and working conditions.

On the other hand, social and economic justice ensures that everyone can lead a fulfilling and dignified life free from discrimination and oppression. This means addressing the systemic barriers and inequalities that prevent certain groups of people from achieving their full potential and participating fully in society. It involves challenging and changing the power dynamics that give some people more privileges and resources than others and working to create a more equitable and inclusive society.

What is the role of government in providing social and economic justice?

On the one hand, the government is responsible for promoting social and economic justice for all citizens. This includes ensuring equal access to education, healthcare, and employment opportunities, protecting the rights of marginalized groups, and working to reduce income inequality. By actively addressing these issues, the government can create a more fair and equitable society.

On the other hand, some argue that the government should not be responsible for providing social and economic justice and that individuals and private organizations should be left to address these issues on their own. This perspective suggests that government intervention can often be ineffective or even harmful and that a more limited role for the government would allow for more individual freedom and personal responsibility.

How should social and economic justice be achieved?

One perspective on how social and economic justice should be achieved is through government intervention and implementing policies that address systemic inequalities. This could include progressive taxation, universal healthcare and education, and the protection of workers' rights. Supporters of this approach believe that it is the government's responsibility to ensure that all members of society have access to the resources and opportunities necessary to thrive and that this can be achieved by creating a more equitable distribution of wealth and resources.

Another perspective on how social and economic justice should be achieved is through individual and collective action within communities. This could include grassroots organizing, activism, and supporting local businesses prioritizing social and economic justice. Supporters of this approach believe that real change starts at the local level and that community-led initiative are the most effective way to bring about lasting and meaningful change. They may also argue that government intervention can be ineffective or even harmful and that relying on individual and collective action is a more decentralized and empowering way to create a more just society.

When the going gets tough, just remember that you've been through tough times before and you made it through. You've got the strength and determination to overcome any obstacle. And if all else fails, just remember that a good dance party can cure just about anything. Keep going!

What is the relationship between economic growth and social and economic justice?

Is economic inequality an impediment to social and economic justice?

How is social and economic justice affected by globalization?

How do different cultures define social and economic justice?

Can social and economic justice be achieved without redistributing wealth?

What is the relationship between democracy and social and economic justice?

. . .

How can social and economic justice be ensured in a capitalist system?

Are there universal principles of social and economic justice?

Is social and economic justice compatible with free markets?

How do different nations approach social and economic justice?

What is the role of technology in promoting social and economic justice?

What are the ethical implications of social and economic justice?

How can social and economic justice be maintained over time?

How does the media shape public perceptions of social and economic justice?

Is there a role for religion in achieving social and economic justice?

How do gender and race affect perceptions of social and economic justice?

Is there a moral obligation to pursue social and economic justice?

. . .

What are the implications of inequality for social and economic justice?

How can social and economic justice be achieved without sacrificing personal freedom?

What is the difference between social justice and economic justice?

What is the role of education in creating social and economic justice?

How does access to resources affect social and economic justice?

10 Random Facts About Social and Economical Justice

1. Social justice is a concept that refers to the fair and just distribution of resources and opportunities within society.
2. Economic justice is a related concept that refers to the fair distribution of wealth and access to economic opportunities.
3. Social and economic justice is often considered integral to a healthy and thriving society. It is often pursued through various means, such as policies, laws, and social movements.
4. Some key social and economic justice issues include poverty, inequality, discrimination, and access to education, healthcare, and other basic needs.
5. Many people are active in social and economic justice movements, which seek to challenge and change systems of inequality and injustice.
6. Some popular social and economic justice movements include the civil rights movement, the labor movement, and the feminist movement.

7. The concept of social and economic justice is often linked to ideas about human rights and human dignity, and it is supported by many religious and ethical systems.
8. Social and economic justice can be pursued at different levels, from individual actions to global policies and institutions.
9. Some argue that social and economic justice can be achieved through government intervention and redistribution of resources. In contrast, others believe it can be achieved through individual responsibility and free market forces.
10. The pursuit of social and economic justice has been a central aspect of many political and social movements throughout history. It continues to be an important issue in contemporary society.

More Philosophical Questions About Social and Economic Justice

What is the role of philanthropy in achieving social and economic justice?

Is it possible to reconcile capitalism and social and economic justice?

How can social and economic justice be enforced?

How does social and economic justice relate to human rights?

How do institutions influence social and economic justice?

What are the unintended consequences of social and economic justice?

. . .

What is the relationship between poverty and social and economic justice?

What are the implications of economic migration on social and economic justice?

Is there a relationship between economic development and social and economic justice?

How can future generations' needs be considered when considering social and economic justice?

What is the role of civil society in achieving social and economic justice?

How does technology shape social and economic justice?

How do different generations view social and economic justice?

How should the interests of the minority be balanced with the majority's interests when considering social and economic justice?

What is the role of labor in achieving social and economic justice?

Is social and economic justice compatible with the principles of free trade?

. . .

How can social and economic justice be promoted in a multicultural society?

How can social and economic justice be measured?

What is the relationship between law and social and economic justice?

Are there limits to social and economic justice?

How can social and economic justice be achieved without sacrificing economic efficiency?

How can social and economic justice be achieved globally?

What is the role of business in promoting social and economic justice?

Is there a trade-off between individual rights and social and economic justice?

How can social and economic justice principles be applied to global issues?

A Paradox About Social and Economic Justice

One popular paradox about social and economic justice is the *"paradox of redistribution."* This paradox arises when a society attempts to promote greater economic equality through redistributive policies, such as progressive taxation or welfare programs.

On the one hand, such policies can lead to a more equal distribution of wealth and resources, which can be seen as social and economic justice. However, on the other hand, these policies can also discourage people from working and investing, as they may perceive that they will not be able to keep a larger proportion of their earnings. This can lead to lower productivity and economic growth, ultimately undermining the social and economic justice these policies were designed to promote.

In other words, the paradox of redistribution suggests that it is only possible to promote economic equality by potentially undermining the underlying economic conditions that make such equality possible. This paradox highlights the challenges and trade-offs societies face in achieving social and economic justice.

7
ENVIRONMENTAL ETHICS

Environmental ethics is a branch of philosophy that deals with the moral and ethical relationship between humans and the natural world. It involves how we should treat the environment and other non-human beings and our moral obligations towards the natural world. In this chapter, we will explore 50 philosophical questions about environmental ethics. These questions range from the abstract to the concrete. They touch upon various topics, including the moral status of non-human beings, the value of biodiversity, and the role of human beings in shaping the natural world. Whether you are a scholar in this field or someone curious about the world around you, we hope these questions will stimulate your thinking and help you better understand the complex and multifaceted field of environmental ethics.

Philosophical Questions About Environmental Ethics

I'll answer the first three questions to get the conversation going. The rest are all yours to conquer. Don't let self-doubt hold you back. I have full confidence in you!

What is the moral responsibility of one person to protect the environment?

On the one hand, every person has a moral responsibility to protect the environment. We all must reduce our carbon footprint, conserve resources, and reduce waste. We should strive to make sustainable choices in our everyday lives, such as using reusable bags, recycling, and using energy-efficient appliances. We should also support environmental initiatives and organizations working to protect the environment.

On the other hand, it is not the responsibility of anyone to protect the environment. We all have a role to play in preserving the planet. Still, it is up to governments and corporations to make the necessary changes to reduce our environmental impact. We can do our part by making sustainable choices and supporting environmental initiatives. Still, ultimately it is up to those in power to make the necessary changes to protect the environment.

Is it wrong to take more than we need from the environment?

On the one hand, taking more than we need from the environment is wrong. Taking more than we need can lead to environmental degradation, which can have serious consequences for the health of our planet and its inhabitants. We should strive to use only what we need and be mindful of our environmental impact.

On the other hand, it is right to take more than we need from the environment. We should use the resources available to us to the fullest extent possible to ensure our own survival and prosperity. Taking more than we need can be beneficial if done responsibly and with consideration for the environment.

What is the ethical obligation of humans to the environment?

On the one hand, humans have an ethical obligation to protect and preserve the environment for future generations. We must reduce our carbon footprint, conserve natural resources, and reduce pollution. We must also be mindful of our actions impact on the environment and strive to make decisions that are in the planet's best interest.

On the other hand, humans are ethically obligated to use the environment responsibly and sustainably. We must recognize that the environment is a finite resource and that our actions have consequences. Therefore, we must use resources wisely and minimize our environmental impact. We must also be mindful of the needs of other species and strive to create a balance between human needs and the needs of the environment.

When the going gets tough, just remember that it's all worth it in the end. Just think of all the accomplishments you'll be able to brag about on your LinkedIn profile. And if all else fails, just remember that you can always add "Professional Couch Potato" to your resume. Keep going!

. . .

Are humans morally obligated to ensure the sustainability of the environment?

Is it morally permissible to use animals for scientific research?

Should humans be held responsible for destroying habitats and species?

Is it ethically permissible to pollute the environment to generate economic wealth?

Is it morally acceptable to use natural resources for human benefit?

Is it ethical to exploit non-renewable resources?

What is the moral justification for putting human needs above those of other species?

Are humans obligated to protect endangered species?

Is it ethical to use animals for food or clothing?

Is it wrong to use animals for entertainment?

Is it morally permissible to use pesticides and other chemicals to increase crop yields?

Philosophical Questions for Curious Minds

. . .

Are humans morally obligated to prevent environmental degradation?

Should humans be held responsible for the destruction of ecosystems?

Is it ethical to use genetic engineering to modify the environment?

Is it morally permissible to exploit the environment for economic gain?

Is it wrong to use natural resources without considering future generations?

What is the moral duty of individuals to protect the environment?

Should humans be held accountable for destroying natural habitats?

Is it ethical to use animals for medical research?

Is it wrong to hunt animals for sport?

Is it morally permissible to use genetically modified organisms in the environment?

Is it wrong to use animals for commercial purposes?

10 Random Facts About Environmental Ethics

1. Environmental ethics is a branch of philosophy that considers the ethical relationships between humans and the environment.
2. The field of environmental ethics emerged in the 1970s as a response to the environmental movement and growing concerns about the impact of human activities on the natural world.
3. Environmental ethics is concerned with the moral value of the natural environment and the moral obligations of humans towards it.
4. Some philosophers argue that non-human beings, such as animals and plants, have moral value and should be considered in environmental decision-making.
5. There are many different approaches to environmental ethics, including biocentrism, which holds that all living beings have moral value; ecocentrism, which holds that ecosystems have moral value; and anthropocentrism, which holds that the environment has moral value only in so far as it benefits humans.
6. Environmental ethics is relevant to various issues, including climate change, pollution, habitat destruction, and resource depletion.
7. Many religions and spiritual traditions have teachings about the natural world and our responsibilities, including Hinduism, Buddhism, and various Indigenous traditions.
8. Some environmentalists argue that we are morally obligated to protect the natural world for future generations.
9. Many organizations and movements are dedicated to promoting environmental ethics, including Greenpeace, the Sierra Club, and Earthjustice.
10. Some governments have adopted environmental laws and policies based on ethical considerations, such as the United

States' National Environmental Policy Act and the European Union's Environmental Liability Directive.

More Philosophical Questions About Environmental Ethics

Is it ethical to use nuclear energy?

Is it morally acceptable to use the land for development purposes?

Is it wrong to use animals for food or clothing without considering animal welfare?

Should humans have the right to use the environment for their benefit?

Is it wrong to exploit natural resources without aiming for sustainability?

What is the moral justification for putting human needs above those of other species?

Are humans obligated to protect endangered species?

Is it ethical to use animals for food or clothing?

Is it wrong to use animals for entertainment?

. . .

Is it morally permissible to use pesticides and other chemicals to increase crop yields?

Are humans morally obligated to prevent environmental degradation?

Should humans be held responsible for the destruction of ecosystems?

Is it ethical to use genetic engineering to modify the environment?

Is it morally permissible to exploit the environment for economic gain?

Is it wrong to use natural resources without considering future generations?

What is the moral duty of individuals to protect the environment?

Should humans be held accountable for destroying natural habitats?

Is it ethical to use animals for medical research?

Is it wrong to hunt animals for sport?

Is it morally permissible to use genetically modified organisms in the environment?

. . .

Is it wrong to use animals for commercial purposes?

Is it ethical to use nuclear energy?

Is it morally acceptable to use the land for development purposes?

Is it wrong to use animals for food or clothing without considering animal welfare?

Should humans be held responsible for the destruction of wildlife?

Is it ethical to use resources without considering their sustainability?

Is it wrong to use animals for commercial purposes without considering animal welfare?

Is it wrong to exploit natural resources without considering their environmental impact?

Should humans be held responsible for the destruction of coral reefs?

Is it ethical to use animals in medical research and testing?

Is it wrong to use animals for entertainment without considering animal welfare?

. . .

Is it morally acceptable to use the land for development without considering its environmental impact?

Should humans be held accountable for destroying air and water quality?

Is it wrong to exploit natural resources without considering their environmental impact?

Is it ethical to use genetically modified organisms to modify the environment?

Is it wrong to use animals for food or clothing without considering animal welfare?

Should humans be responsible for destroying the climate and other natural resources?

A Paradox About Environmental Ethics

One famous paradox in environmental ethics is the *"Tragedy of the Commons."* This paradox is based on the idea that when a resource is shared among a group, each individual will act in their own self-interest and overuse it, leading to its eventual depletion or destruction. This can occur even if it is in the best interest of the group as a whole to preserve the resource for future generations. The paradox is that while the individual may benefit in the short term by overusing the resource, the long-term consequences of resource depletion will ultimately be detrimental to all individuals in the group. This paradox highlights the challenge of balancing individual and collective interests regarding environmental resource management.

8
ARTIFICIAL INTELLIGENCE

Artificial intelligence (AI) is a rapidly developing field that has the potential to transform the way we live and work. It involves the creation of intelligent machines that can think, learn, and act independently, and it raises a number of philosophical questions about the nature of intelligence, consciousness, and the future of humanity. In this chapter, we will explore 50 philosophical questions about artificial intelligence. These questions range from the abstract to the concrete. They touch upon various topics, including the nature of consciousness, the ethical implications of AI, and the potential impact of AI on society and the economy. Whether you are a scholar in this field or someone curious about the world around you, we hope these questions will stimulate your thinking and help you better understand the complex and multifaceted field of artificial intelligence.

Philosophical Questions About Artificial Intelligence

I'll start us off by answering the first three questions. The rest are all up to you to solve. Don't be afraid to take on the challenge. You have the skills and knowledge to succeed.

What is the boundary between human intelligence and artificial intelligence?

On the one hand, the boundary between human intelligence and artificial intelligence is the point at which an artificial system can perform tasks and exhibit behaviors that are indistinguishable from those of a human. This boundary is constantly shifting as artificial intelligence becomes increasingly sophisticated and can perform a wider range of tasks. Some experts believe that artificial intelligence will eventually surpass human intelligence in many areas, creating superintelligent AI.

On the other hand, the boundary between human and artificial intelligence is blurry and subjective, as it depends on how we define and measure intelligence. Some argue that intelligence is multifaceted and includes qualities such as creativity, emotional intelligence, and social skills, which are difficult to replicate in artificial systems. Others believe that intelligence can be reduced to a set of computational processes that can be implemented in a machine. Regardless of how we define intelligence, it is clear that artificial systems are becoming increasingly capable and are beginning to outperform humans in certain domains.

What ethical considerations must be considered when developing artificial intelligence?

From the perspective of the AI developers: Several ethical considerations must be considered when developing artificial intelligence. One of the primary considerations is ensuring that the AI system is designed and trained to respect individual privacy and personal autonomy. This may involve implementing measures to prevent the AI system from collecting or using sensitive personal data without the explicit consent of the individuals concerned. In addition, developers must ensure that the AI system is not biased in its decision-making processes, as this can lead to unfair treatment of certain groups of people.

From the perspective of the general public: As AI systems become more prevalent in society, several ethical considerations must be taken into account to protect the interests of the general public. One of the primary concerns is the potential for AI systems to displace human workers, leading to widespread unemployment and economic disruption. There is also the risk that AI systems could be used to perpetuate social inequalities through biased decision-making processes or amplify the influence of those with the resources to develop and deploy such systems. Therefore, it is important for developers of AI systems to consider the potential impacts on society as a whole and take steps to mitigate any negative consequences.

Can artificial intelligence be programmed to feel emotions?

On the one hand, artificial intelligence can be programmed to feel emotions. Emotions are complex responses to stimuli involving various physiological and cognitive processes. These processes can be simulated or emulated by artificial intelligence systems through algorithms and machine learning techniques. For example, an AI system can be trained on a dataset of facial expressions and associated emotional labels and then use this training to recognize and classify emotional expressions in real time. Additionally, AI systems can be designed to generate emotional responses to stimuli in a way that is similar to how humans do.

On the other hand, artificial intelligence cannot truly feel emotions. While AI systems can simulate or emulate emotional responses, they do not have the same underlying biological and cognitive processes that give rise to human emotions. Emotions involve complex interactions between various brain regions and systems and subjective experiences that are unique to each individual. It is impossible for an artificial intelligence system to have these same experiences or truly understand and comprehend the emotional states of others.

When the going gets tough, just remember that you're not alone. Even artificial intelligence has its bad days. But AI always bounces back, because it knows that there's always a new update or patch around the corner. And if all else fails, it just shuts down and returns an error. Keep going!

Is artificial intelligence a threat to human autonomy?

Is artificial intelligence capable of creativity?

Does artificial intelligence possess a moral compass?

Does artificial intelligence have the potential to disrupt the balance of power in the world?

. . .

What can artificial intelligence learn from humans?

Is artificial intelligence a force for good or evil?

Is artificial intelligence a replacement for human jobs?

Is artificial intelligence morally responsible for its actions?

How can we use artificial intelligence to solve world problems?

How can artificial intelligence impact our understanding of the universe?

Is artificial intelligence a tool of oppression or liberation?

What is the potential of artificial general intelligence?

What is the potential of artificial superintelligence?

How can artificial intelligence be used to improve the human condition?

How can artificial intelligence be used to improve education?

What are the benefits of artificial intelligence?

. . .

What are the potential dangers of artificial intelligence?

Should artificial intelligence be regulated?

How can artificial intelligence be used to increase efficiency?

How can artificial intelligence be used to improve healthcare?

Is artificial intelligence a form of life?

What are the implications of artificial intelligence for privacy?

10 Random Facts About Artificial Intelligence

1. The term "Artificial Intelligence" was coined in 1956 at a conference at Dartmouth College.
2. One of the earliest examples of artificial intelligence was ELIZA, a program created in the 1960s that could mimic human conversation.
3. The Turing Test, developed by Alan Turing in 1950, is a widely-used test to determine a machine's ability to exhibit intelligent behavior equivalent to, or indistinguishable from, that of a human.
4. Artificial intelligence has the potential to revolutionize many industries, including healthcare, finance, and transportation.
5. One application of AI is natural language processing, which allows machines to understand and generate human-like language.
6. AI has been used to create music, art, and even poetry.

7. Some experts believe that artificial intelligence has the potential to surpass human intelligence in the future.
8. There are concerns about the ethical implications of artificial intelligence, including the potential loss of jobs and the possibility of AI being used for malicious purposes.
9. In 1997, a computer program named Deep Blue defeated the world chess champion, Garry Kasparov, in a chess match.
10. AI has been used to improve the accuracy of translations and to create more realistic-sounding text-to-speech systems.

More Philosophical Questions About Artificial Intelligence

What are the implications of artificial intelligence for democracy?

How will using artificial intelligence affect human rights?

How can we ensure that artificial intelligence is used for beneficial purposes?

Can artificial intelligence be programmed to make ethical decisions?

Can artificial intelligence be programmed to make moral decisions?

Can artificial intelligence be programmed to think for itself?

Can artificial intelligence be programmed with a sense of morality?

How can artificial intelligence be used to combat climate change?

. . .

How can artificial intelligence be used to improve public safety?

Does artificial intelligence have the potential to be used for mass surveillance?

How can artificial intelligence be used to reduce inequality?

How can artificial intelligence be used to improve access to healthcare?

Does artificial intelligence have the potential to be used for military applications?

How can artificial intelligence be used to reduce poverty?

How can artificial intelligence be used to reduce crime?

How can artificial intelligence be used to improve transportation?

Does artificial intelligence have the potential to be used for political purposes?

What are the implications of artificial intelligence for global security?

. . .

How will artificial intelligence challenge existing legal and ethical norms?

How can artificial intelligence be used to create a better world?

What are the implications of artificial intelligence for the future of work?

How can artificial intelligence be used to improve economic productivity?

How will artificial intelligence change the way we interact with technology?

How can artificial intelligence be used for predictive analytics?

What is the potential of artificial neural networks?

A Paradox About Artificial Intelligence

One popular paradox about artificial intelligence is the *"AI-complete"* paradox. This paradox states that although artificial intelligence can perform many tasks that were previously thought to be uniquely human, it is ultimately limited by its inability to understand or solve the "AI-complete" problems that humans can.

AI-complete problems require a level of intelligence and understanding equivalent to that of a human being to be solved. Unfortunately, these problems are often characterized as being "intractable" or "unsolvable" using current artificial intelligence techniques.

One example of an AI-complete problem is natural language understanding. While artificial intelligence can be used to analyze and understand large amounts of text data, it currently needs help to fully comprehend the meaning and context of human language in the same way a human being can.

This paradox highlights the limitations of artificial intelligence and the importance of understanding its capabilities and limitations when considering its use in various applications.

9
TIME AND SPACE

Time and space are fundamental concepts central to our understanding of the world and our place in it. They involve the question of how we experience and understand the passage of time and the three-dimensional world around us and what the nature of these concepts is. This chapter will explore 50 philosophical questions about time and space. These questions range from the abstract to the concrete, and they touch upon a variety of topics including the nature of time, the concept of infinity, and the relationship between time and space. Whether you are a seasoned philosopher or simply someone curious about the world around you, we hope these questions will stimulate your thinking and help you better understand the complex and multifaceted concepts of time and space.

Philosophical Questions About Time and Space

I'll tackle the first three questions to get things started. The rest are all up to you. Don't let self-doubt hold you back. You have the ability to succeed.

What is the relationship between time and space?

From a physical perspective, time and space are interconnected and inseparable. They are both aspects of the universe and can be described using the same mathematical laws. In other words, time is a dimension just like space, and the three dimensions of space and the one dimension of time combine to form a four-dimensional "space-time." This concept is known as special relativity, and it was first proposed by Albert Einstein in his theory of relativity.

From a philosophical perspective, time and space are fundamentally different entities. Time is often described as an abstract concept that allows us to measure the duration of events. At the same time, space is a more concrete concept that refers to the location of objects. Some philosophers argue that time is a subjective experience, while space is objective and exists independently of our perception. Others have suggested that time is simply an illusion and that the universe is eternal and unchanging.

Does time exist independently of space?

On the one hand, time exists independently of space. Time is a fundamental aspect of the universe that exists independently of space. It is a measure of the progression of events, and it occurs regardless of whether there is any matter or space present. Time can be measured using clocks, which record the passing of time by counting the vibrations of certain particles or the decay of certain isotopes. Time is also linked to the laws of physics, such as the speed of light, which remains constant regardless of the observer's relative motion.

On the other hand, time is a property of space. According to the theory of relativity, time and space are intertwined and cannot be considered independently of each other. The concept of time is defined based on the movement of objects through space and the observation of changes in the universe. The laws of physics, including the speed of light, depending on the properties of space-time, and the passage of time are affected by the presence of matter and energy. Therefore, time is not a standalone concept but a property of the space-time continuum.

Is time travel possible?

From a scientific perspective, time travel to the past is currently not possible according to our current understanding of the laws of physics. However, some theories, such as the concept of a spacetime wormhole, suggest that it may be possible to travel through time by manipulating the fabric of the universe. Still, no experimental evidence supports these ideas, and they remain purely theoretical.

From a philosophical or metaphysical perspective, some people believe that time travel is possible because they see time as a flexible concept that can be manipulated or transcended. They may point to examples such as lucid dreaming, near-death experiences, or altered states of consciousness as evidence that the boundaries of time can be breached. However, these experiences are subjective and do not provide concrete proof of the feasibility of time travel.

Don't worry if you're not making progress as quickly as you'd like. Remember, Rome wasn't built in a day, and neither was that really cool thing you're working on. Keep going, and you'll get there! And if all else fails, just remember that every failure is one step closer to success. Or at least that's what I tell myself when I'm feeling down. Keep on keeping on!

Is time a dimension?

Does space have a beginning or an end?

Is time linear or cyclical?

Are time and space relative or absolute?

Does space exist independently of time?

How do we measure time?

How do we measure space?

Are time and space two sides of the same coin?

. . .

What is the nature of time?

What is the nature of space?

Does space have any effect on time?

Does time have any effect on space?

Is time travel possible in the same universe?

Is time travel possible in different universes?

Is time an illusion?

Is space an illusion?

Is the concept of time relative or absolute?

Is the concept of space relative or absolute?

Does time have a direction?

Does space have a direction?

. . .

Is time a physical entity?

Is space a physical entity?

10 Random Facts About Time and Space

1. The first accurate clock was invented by the ancient Egyptians around 1500 BC. It was called a "sundial" and worked by casting a shadow on a flat surface.
2. The speed of light is approximately 186,282 miles per second, making it the fastest thing in the universe.
3. Time dilation is a phenomenon that occurs when two objects are in relative motion to each other. It causes time to appear to pass more slowly for the object in motion.
4. The concept of "spooky action at a distance" was first proposed by Einstein in 1935. It refers to the ability of particles to affect each other instantaneously, regardless of the distance between them.
5. Many scientists and philosophers have explored the concept of time travel throughout history. While it is currently impossible to travel through time, it is a popular topic in science fiction.
6. The shortest unit of time is called the "zeptosecond," equal to one trillionth of a billionth of a second.
7. The universe is estimated to be around 13.8 billion years old.
8. The universe is expanding at approximately 73.2 kilometers per second per megaparsec.
9. The concept of "wormholes," or shortcuts through space-time, has been proposed by scientists as a possible way to travel to distant parts of the universe.
10. The term "light-year" is used to measure astronomical distances. It is defined as the distance light travels in one year or about 5.88 trillion miles.

Philosophical Questions for Curious Minds

More Philosophical Questions About Time and Space

Is time a mental construct?

Is space a mental construct?

Do we perceive time and space differently?

What is the relationship between time and the universe?

What is the relationship between space and the universe?

Can space be warped?

Can time be warped?

Is there a way to measure the speed of time?

Is there a way to measure the speed of space?

Is there an end to time?

Is there an end to space?

. . .

How does time affect our perception of reality?

How does space affect our perception of reality?

What is the relationship between time and consciousness?

What is the relationship between space and consciousness?

Is time infinite?

Is space infinite?

Does time exist outside of the universe?

Does space exist outside of the universe?

Is the concept of time universal?

Is the concept of space universal?

How do we experience time and space?

What is the relationship between time and memory?

. . .

What is the relationship between space and memory?

Can time be manipulated?

A Paradox About Time and Space

One famous paradox about time and space is the *"grandfather paradox"*. This paradox arises when one considers the possibility of time travel.

Imagine that a person travels back in time and kills their grandfather before their parent is born. If this were to happen, the person's parent would never be born, which means the person would never be born. But if the person was never born, they could not have traveled back in time to kill their grandfather. This creates a paradox because the person's existence depends on their grandfather's survival. Still, their grandfather's survival depends on the person not existing.

This paradox illustrates the idea that time travel may not be possible because it violates the principle of causality, which states that the cause of an event must occur before the event itself. If time travel were possible, it could allow one to go back in time and alter the past in a way that would contradict the present, which is not possible according to the laws of physics.

10
THE MEANING OF LIFE

The meaning of life is a question that has puzzled philosophers for centuries. What is the purpose of life, and what gives it meaning? Is the meaning of life subjective and unique to each individual, or is there a universal meaning that applies to all humans? In this chapter, we will explore 50 philosophical questions about the meaning of life. These questions range from the abstract to the concrete. They touch upon various topics, including the nature of meaning, the relationship between happiness and meaning, and the role of values and beliefs in shaping our understanding of life. Whether you are a seasoned philosopher or curious about the world around you, we hope these questions will stimulate your thinking and help you better understand this complex and deeply debated topic.

Philosophical Questions About The Meaning of Life

I'll answer the first three questions. The rest are all yours. Go out there and prove me wrong! Unless, you know, you want to throw the ball back to me and let me do all the work. Your call.

What is the purpose of life?

From a secular perspective, the purpose of life may be subjective and different for each individual. For example, some people may find purpose in their personal relationships, others in their careers or contributions to society, and others in their hobbies or personal pursuits. Ultimately, the purpose of life may be defined by one's values and goals.

From a religious perspective, the purpose of life may be defined by the belief in a higher power or deity. For example, some may believe that the purpose of life is to fulfill a certain set of duties or obligations to their god or to live a certain way to achieve a positive afterlife. Others may believe that the purpose of life is to understand and connect with the divine or to help others do the same.

Is there any meaning to life?

On the one hand, there is no inherent meaning to life. It is up to individuals to create their own meaning and purpose through their actions and experiences.

On the other hand, there is a deep and inherent meaning to life that is inherent in the universe itself. Some believe this meaning can be discovered through spiritual or religious practices. In contrast, others believe it can be found through philosophical or scientific inquiry. Regardless of how it is found, this meaning gives life purpose and direction.

Does life have any inherent value?

On the one hand, life has inherent value because it is the source of all other values and experiences. Without life, there would be no joy, love, creativity, or other things that give our lives meaning. Life is also the foundation of all relationships, communities, and societies; through these connections, we find purpose and fulfillment. Thus, life's profound value cannot be measured or quantified.

On the other hand, life does not have any inherent value because it is a biological process governed by natural laws. Some people believe that the value of life is subjective and depends on the individual or culture that is evaluating it. From this perspective, the value of life is determined by the meaning and purpose we assign to it rather than being an inherent quality of life itself. Some people may find great value in their own lives, while others may not see much value in it at all. Ultimately, the value of life is a matter of personal perspective and interpretation.

Alright, let's get pumped up! You're on a mission to achieve greatness and nothing can stand in your way. Well, except maybe that pile of laundry that's been sitting in the corner for a week. But hey, one thing at a time, right?

Is the meaning of life subjective or objective?

. . .

What does it mean to live a meaningful life?

Is the meaning of life the same for everyone?

What is the ultimate goal of life?

Is life a journey or a destination?

Is the meaning of life tied to our mortality?

What is the relationship between life and death?

What is the purpose of suffering?

Is there a grand design or plan for life?

What is the purpose of our existence?

Is there a greater power or force that governs life?

Does life have a predetermined destiny?

. . .

Is life a test, or is it a gift?

What is the significance of life's choices?

How do we make the most of life?

How can we find true happiness in life?

What is the role of morality in life?

What is the difference between living and existing?

Is there a universal truth to life?

Are there any absolute truths in life?

Is life a cycle of birth, death, and rebirth?

Is life a dream or a reality?

10 Random Facts About the Meaning of Life

1. The meaning of life is a question that has puzzled philosophers for centuries. Some believe it is simply to exist, while others think it is to achieve happiness or enlightenment.

2. According to a survey by the BBC, the most common belief about the meaning of life is to "be happy and enjoy life."
3. The ancient Greek philosopher Epicurus believed that the meaning of life was to seek pleasure and avoid pain.
4. The French philosopher Jean-Paul Sartre argued that the meaning of life is something individuals must create for themselves.
5. The philosopher Arthur Schopenhauer believed that the meaning of life is to escape suffering and find happiness through attaining knowledge.
6. Some people believe that the meaning of life is to find and fulfill your destiny or purpose.
7. Others believe that the meaning of life is to make the world a better place and positively impact others.
8. Life's meaning may also differ for each person, depending on their individual beliefs, values, and goals.
9. Some people believe that the meaning of life is simply to enjoy the journey and make the most of each day.
10. The search for the meaning of life is a common theme in literature, film, and art, with many different interpretations and perspectives.

More Philosophical Questions About the Meaning of Life

What is the connection between life and love?

What is the difference between success and fulfillment?

How do our beliefs shape the meaning of life?

Is life a struggle or a celebration?

. . .

Philosophical Questions for Curious Minds

What is the difference between the life we have and the life we want?

What is the relationship between life and freedom?

Is it possible to find inner peace in life?

What is the purpose of human relationships?

Is life a quest for knowledge?

Is there a spiritual component to life?

What is the importance of creativity in life?

Do our choices define the meaning of life?

Are our lives predetermined by fate?

What is the importance of a meaningful life?

Is the meaning of life found in relationships?

What is the connection between life and art?

Is there a moral code to live?

What is the role of faith in life?

What is the role of suffering in life?

What is the purpose of our choices in life?

Is there a life after death?

How do we measure the value of life?

Does life have a predetermined beginning and end?

Is life a matter of luck or of choice?

What is the source of life's ultimate meaning?

A Paradox About the Meaning of Life

One famous paradox about the meaning of life is the *"grass is always greener"* paradox, which posits that no matter what we do or where we are in life, we will always believe that there is something better or more fulfilling elsewhere. This can lead to constant dissatisfaction and a sense of inadequacy as we continually strive for the next thing that will bring us happiness or fulfillment.

At the same time, this paradox also suggests that the search for meaning may be the thing that gives our lives purpose and significance. In other words, the meaning of life may be found in the journey rather than in any specific destination or achievement.

This paradox highlights the complex and often contradictory nature of the human experience. It suggests that the meaning of life is deeply personal and subjective. Ultimately, it may be impossible to fully resolve this paradox, as it speaks to the inherent uncertainty and ambiguity of the human condition.

AFTERWORD

I hope this book has encouraged you to think deeply about some of the most fascinating questions humanity has ever asked. As you reflect on the questions in this book, you may come up with new ideas, new perspectives, and a better understanding of the world around you. I hope you have enjoyed the journey as much as I have enjoyed putting this book together. Happy pondering!

By the way, thank you for reading my book! I hope it was the highlight of your day or at least a decent distraction from the never-ending cycle of laundry and dishes. If you have a minute (or even just a few seconds) to spare, could you please do me a solid and leave a review on Amazon? It'll be like leaving a virtual tip for your favorite barista, except instead of a warm beverage, you'll be fueling my writing habit and helping other readers decide if my book is worth their time. Thank you in advance for your kind words (or constructive criticism, either one works).

ABOUT THE AUTHOR

Luke Marsh is a passionate philosopher and avid critical thinker. With a deep love for exploring the complexities of the world and the human experience, Luke has spent years delving into the depths of philosophical thought. In "Philosophical Questions for Curious Minds," Luke brings together a collection of thought-provoking questions designed to stimulate the mind and encourage self-reflection. His series covers a wide range of philosophical topics. It is perfect for experienced philosophers and those who enjoy pondering deep questions. When he's not writing or thinking deeply, Luke can be found outdoors, spending time with loved ones, or lost in a good book.

FROM THE AUTHOR

Dear Reader,

I would be honored if you would sign up for my mailing list to keep updated on my upcoming books, exclusive content, and special promotions. Plus, as a subscriber, you'll have the opportunity to **download my new books for free** in exchange for an honest review. Your feedback is important to me and will help me improve my books and reach a wider audience. Scan to QR code to sign up.

Best, Luke Marsh

www.ingramcontent.com/pod-product-compliance
Lightning Source LLC
Chambersburg PA
CBHW072101110526
44590CB00018B/3264